Motherhood

The course of birth

By

Sarah Alfred

List of Contents

Chapter VII: The Functions of an Aunt or Uncle

Chapter 1

Introduction

Who is a mother?

The only woman in the world who will still **cradle** you in her arms even if you've stabbed her loving heart each time you've **hung up** her calls, thrown away her delicious food just because your friends thought fast food was cool; got a red-ink stained **progress report**; told her to go away in the presence of your apparently 'cool' friends, ignored her for telling you to do your school work before play; taking juvenile revenge on her

for only protecting you from the seemingly harmless evils in the world around you.
And still say she loves you and you will always be her child, no matter what.
It's not just the ***placenta*** *that forms a bond between a mother and a child. It's the mother herself who loves her child unconditionally.*
The most amazing, strong, loving, and **heroic** woman you will ever know. She gets up earlier and stays up later than anyone else and still manages to keep the family together. She teaches you the things you can't learn from anyone else through examples and **hard work**.
Often punishes you for things you don't think are fair as a child but **grow**

up to appreciate the character she helped you build.

A mother plays the most important roles in our lives. A mother's role starts from being pregnant and maintaining a human life for nine months and eventually giving birth to the child with the risk of losing her life. Giving birth is just the beginning of a mother's complex and significant role in raising a family throughout her life.

Chapter 2

Responsibilities of a mother

A mother's central responsibility is to protect and nurture her children and help them grow up to become productive human

beings. The amount of responsibility that a mother has often depends on the state of her household and whether or not she has a partner to aid her.
A mother is chiefly responsible for nurturing and rearing her children. A mother has an obligation to help her children develop strong moral principles early in life. The mother's presence and daily guidance in the lives of her children helps them to develop positive character traits with love and compassion for others.
A mother who shirks her responsibilities to her children may encourage them to go on a wayward, destructive path in life. Mothers must also correct children when they do

something wrong to teach them how to do better.
A mother cannot prevent her children from experiencing every type of pain and hardship, but her kind and compassionate words can soften the blows of life.
Modern mothers who are single parents are expected to take on greater roles and responsibilities in the lives of their children, but some have family members to help them out.

Being a mother is not easy as you will have to shoulder a lot of responsibilities.
For a mother, her child is her world and she plays a very important role in the growth and development of her child. All mothers have to fulfill important

parenting duties and responsibilities which help in raising children into happy and successful individuals.

Discussed below are 10 important parenting duties and responsibilities of mothers.

Making Decisions that Are Really Tough

As a mother, sometimes you need to make really difficult decisions, like whether to let your kid complete the difficult chores on his or her own or to force your kid to say sorry after misbehavior and rudeness.

These decisions will probably make your kids hate you temporarily, but you are anyway responsible for taking them.

Building Self-Reliance in Children

As a mother, it is your responsibility to slowly teach your kids to do their own work and ultimately progress towards becoming independent individuals.

Start with teaching how to tie up shoelaces and then move on to self-dealing with criticism and bullying. As time passes, these skills get translated into looking for a job independently and refusing to fall prey to temptation like drugs.

Teaching Accountability

A mom has to be tough at times to teach accountability. When your kids are adamantly watching TV instead of doing their homework, it is

your job to firmly guide them towards their work towards which they are accountable.
Use a polite yet firm voice while explaining issues of accountability.

Be a Pillar of Emotional Support
The bond between mother and child has many shades, but one thing never changes. Kids almost always instinctively turn towards their mother whenever they are in any kind of emotional problem. As a mother it is your responsibility to be the emotional anchor of your children so that they can face the storms of life.

Learn to Say "No"
You may love your kids a lot, but sometimes you have to be responsible

enough to say no to them. This may be applicable in situations when your kids are making unjustified demands or are acting in an unethical manner. Remember that discipline is very necessary for proper moral development and discipline often involves saying "no".

Respecting Boundaries

As a mother, it is very easy to forget that your kids are growing older and wiser. After a time, it becomes necessary for a mother to respect the private space of her children. This may involve not opening private mail, not walking into your kids' rooms without knocking, and eventually letting your kids make their own mistakes.

Teaching the Difference between Right and Wrong

Children are not born with a moral compass and it is the job of parents, especially of the mother, to build that compass for them. Be responsible enough to teach and demonstrate the values that your kids need in order to grow up as decent human beings. You are also responsible for living your life according to the same moral values that you preach, as that is the only way kids will learn.

Smile and go with the flow.

Your responsibility as a mother is to understand that you cannot expect a uniform performance from your child at all times. Life is full of crests and troughs, and when you hit bottom, sometimes you just have to keep a smile on your face and go with the flow.

Love Your Kids

You are responsible for loving your kids even when you realize that they are not perfect. You are responsible for providing pure, unconditional, and unadulterated love that can shield your kids against the world.

Do your best.

As a mother you are responsible for doing your best. At all times and in every situation put in your best effort. After all, sometimes doing your best is all that can be done.

Chapter 3

Roles of a mother

Mother in child-bearing

Child-bearing is the primary and sole responsibility of a mother, as she is the only one who can bear a child. Child-bearing is a very essential responsibility because, without its fulfillment, we won't have a proper family setting of a father, mother, and children.

Mother as a manager.

A mother can also take the role of a manager for the family, considering the numerous dealings a mother must handle in a household. She must not only maintain the physical aspects of her family's life but also the intangible elements, such as creating a lively environment for her husband and children for her entire life.

As a teacher

We can all generally agree that a mother must be able to be a teacher for her children. Mothers must be able to educate their children appropriately by being the best role model they can be for them. This is an important role for a mother in the family. In the process of nurturing the children, the mother ought to teach her children how to behave properly, how to be responsible, and how to indulge in all the aforementioned house chores, from cooking, to how to wash their clothes, to how to wash their plates, amongst others.

Mother as the cook (chef).

A mother must be able to fulfill a family's needs for proper gastronomy starting from when you were a child up to what you are now, an adult. Upon childbearing, it is the responsibility of the mother to cater to such a child. She is solely responsible for breastfeeding that child, and also, as the child grows, she still exercises the responsibility of taking care of the child, carrying the child, and feeding the child.

The same responsibility is still applicable to a mother when she has more than one child. While it is the role of a mother to cater for her child, as expounded above, it is also her traditional duty to do catering for the family. Catering, in this instance, means cooking food, buying foodstuffs, baking snacks, and satisfying the stomachs of members of the family.

My Mother as a Nurse (Caregiver)

Have you ever imagined the tough responsibilities that nurses must endure?

Imagine that role being taken by your mother throughout your life. A mother would monitor what her children would eat, change your diapers when you were a baby,

and dedicate her entire time to looking after her children and husband. In most instances, a mother is caring.
Hence, it is usually her responsibility to exercise care not just for her children but for guests in the house.
That's why most often, when a family receives a visitor, it is usually the mother who runs around gathering refreshments and food that such a visitor will consume.

Mother as the financial controller.
A mother must be able to manage and control her family's financial situation well. The elements that must be managed range from the money spent on basic needs such as food, electricity bills,

recreational plans, and also savings.

Mother as the housekeeper.
Completing house chores has been the traditional role of a mother in the family, hence the emanation of the concept of housewife. A housewife is a woman whose occupation is caring for her family, house affairs, and doing the house chores. This means that in such a family where the mother is a housewife, while the husband goes to work. The mother will stay at home doing the house chores. These chores include but are not limited to: sweeping the house, cooking, washing plates, fetching water, cleaning the house, and washing clothes.

Mother in keeping the family together

With the uprising in divorce cases and judicial separation all over the world, the role of a mother has stepped up as she can now help bring unity and keep the family together through bonding with her children, submitting to her husband, and Childbearing.

Childbearing is a very essential tool of curbing divorce and keeping the family together, as most often the husband will have a double mind with respect to the welfare of their children if there will be a separation, and because of these Children, he will remain committed to the marriage. The mother is usually close to her child.

Hence, she builds a strong emotional bond with such Child and it is, therefore, her duty to inculcate that Child with values, moral principles, and nurture them properly into their environment.

Chapter 4

The Roles of a Teenage Mother

Teenage mothers think and act like teenagers. Just like any other teenager, they can be self-centered and may find it difficult to plan for the future.

Relationships, getting along with parents, and what to do after high school are just a few topics that would provide valuable information to any teenager.

If teenage topics are not discussed and this role of the teenage mother is ignored, teen mothers may conclude that in order to relate to us, they must act more grown up than they are.

While that may sound good at first, there is a down side to acting too mature too quickly. When

a teenage mother is not given the opportunity to address issues that deal with her age, she will push being a teenager to the side for a while.
However, she may revert back to teenage behaviors or situations later in life, often to the detriment of her older child.

The mother

Our society views motherhood as something special. We believe mothers should provide security and stability for their children. A mother must sacrifice many of her own wants and desires for the benefit of her child. But most teens have not reached this level of maturity. She needs to provide herself with the information that will help her become the stable,

mature mother her child requires.
Teenage mothers may want to be good mothers but lack parenting skills. Therefore, she will need to be counseled on how to go about it.

The student

Often, teenage mothers are still in high school. Finishing high school is a critical step toward independence for a teen mom.

They need all the support and, above all, they need to support themselves by believing this is a phase in their lives and it will soon pass. Studying should be done at their own pace with the support of the lecturer/teachers in the school because the female folk react differently to pregnancy emotions and changes.

The employee

Addressing the employee role for the teenage mother may be difficult for many of us. Many believe that it would be best if mothers did not work and instead spent the majority of their time with their children. While this may be the ideal situation, the fact remains that many teenage mothers must work in order to provide for their children. In order to help those mothers who will need to work, family members need to teach them and possibly take them for counseling.

The seeker

Finally, most teenage mothers are either unsaved or have

wandered away from Christ. That they have come to the realization that they need spiritual guidance shows that they are seeking solutions to their problems.
The primary problem for these teen moms is spiritual, even though they may not realize it at first.

The teenage mother's logistical needs may be genuine, but dealing with those needs alone will not solve the primary problem. The teenage mother must be reconciled to Christ before she can experience the healing that comes from forgiveness and find the new purpose and direction she needs. She may choose to respond to the explanation of her need for Christ, or she may disregard it.

Nevertheless, God's Word is powerful, and she may respond to the Gospel message years later.

Chapter 5

Roles of a single mother

A single mother has to endure a lot of problems and face the biggest challenge in her life; being a single parent who must be able to hold multiple roles, that is as a **father who works for a family living and as a mother who nurtures and educates her children.**

Being a mother is the most beautiful and important part of a woman's life. It does not matter how tough the mother's life gets, she always stays positive and supportive with her child and tries to protect her baby from all the problems in the world. Sometimes being a single mother gets tough and hard. We tend to forget ourselves completely in this process, immersed in the duty to provide for our loved ones.

Here are some things you should do to manage your time with your precious one alone on **being a single mother.**

Of course, there is no such thing. I realized that the journey wasn't going to be easy.

A single parent raising children in today's society is definitely the minority.

A single woman raising minority males in today's

society is a greater minority.

How do you beat the odds?

Well, teaching and learning are both initiated in the home. It should be anyway. Infants learn to hold their bottles, crawl, walk, etc. There is nothing that can be taken for granted.

As parents, we can't assume that our children will eventually learn what they need to know from their teachers alone.

Form partnerships with their children's teachers

A child's environment is very important.

Home is always the initial classroom. A baby develops into an infant and then a child. In most

instances, the parents are there.
As parents, it is very important that we start training our children early. The ABC's and 123's have to be enforced when they are infants.
Motor skills, comprehension, etc. can be taught with books, educational toys, educational TV programs, and even everyday household items. All of these things require hands-on, quality time to build the parent-child relationship. If we, as parents, are positioning ourselves to show by example, then our children will mimic what they see.

Exposure is another key factor to learning
Taking advantage of free exhibits, museums, park

activities, library story hours, etc. are all great ideas. A lot of parents want to place the blame on poverty or the economy as a reason why they can't educate their children. These are excuses.

Finding mentors for their children

As a single parent, it is definitely the responsibility of the mother to find the correct mentors and role models for her children. If you don't know, ask somebody. The church is always a great foundation for the development of children. Spiritual exposure when taught early, such as Sunday school, church activities and programs, helps children build their own relationship with God.

Church shouldn't be a place where children are dropped off and picked up.
Parents need to be totally involved in the lives of their children. Whether in church or school, you need to watch how your child interacts with other children and adults. A lot of children don't follow directions because their parents don't follow directions. Once again, showing by example is the best thing we can do as parents. The times of "do as I say and not as I do" are over.

Another key factor in learning is responsibility.
The earlier children learn responsibility, the better. Giving them simple tasks to perform even as small

children helps in their development to be responsible. My son started taking out small bags of garbage every week at the age of three. Later on, they shoveled snow and cut lawns until they were able to work part-time.

A Work Schedule to Suit Your Family

You know how much more hectic it gets when you have to work and manage a baby. You have to give an equal amount of time to your child as well as your work. If you are working from home, stress is a little bit less.

Try to make a schedule that will not affect your family time and your work time. Try to speak to your boss and explain to him/her your problem. so that you can manage your time as well as your job properly. Make him understand your situation and ask for help, like if any of your family members can take care of your child for that particular time, or try to find a trustworthy daycare center where you can keep your child.

Have a Kid-Free Time
We know how much you have to work to make your child happy, and not to make him or her feel any discomfort in life. But sometimes having a kid free time or a simple free time for yourself is needed. With lots of pressure and work taking a day or even a few hours of break can give you a

clear head. You can think or work on the upcoming possibilities and responsibilities, read a book or watch a movie, talk to a friend or family etc.

Do Not Compete with Yourself

You can try to loosen up a bit. When we get up in the morning, we think of what else we have to do the whole day, and we get to work on it. Making the bed, cleaning up the room, cleaning up the dishes, etc. Remember those college days when you used to leave your things messy in your hostel bed and think to yourself, "Who cares?" Well, I am not saying to be entirely like that, but you can take a break from making a bed and do some other important stuff. No one is going to judge you. You do not have to clean the floor every day. Try to invest that time with your child and enjoy every moment.

Always Be Prepared

If you are the mother of a toddler, try to always leave home prepared. Keep things handy whenever you leave. For example, snacks, sippy cups, water, juice boxes, clean clothes, sometimes crayons, coloring books, etc. You do know what your child may require. We might forget sometimes because of busy schedules and work pressure, but it is also important to keep your children busy when you are doing something.

Multitask
As you are already familiar with, as a single mother, you must try to multitask more strategically. You must try to complete your housework while simultaneously spending or playing with your child. In this way, you will have more time to spend with your child. Multitasking is an easy way to manage everything at once.

Chapter 6

Grandparents' roles
Working women have a lot to thank their mothers for. Without the help of their mothers in the home, it would be difficult for young women to balance having a family with advancing in their careers. By taking care of their

daughters' children, grandmothers give their daughters the time they need to work.
Childcare provision leads to a rise in their daughters' labor force participation (LFP). According to research, "Grandparents are the largest source of informal childcare" for working women. In some parts of

Nigeria and in most parts of developed countries like Italy, almost 50 percent of grandparents provide daily care for their grandchildren.
Although passing the responsibility of childcare over to their parents gives women freedom and independence to pursue their careers, it creates a problem for grandmothers.

Grandmothers, rather than young daughters, get saddled with having to balance work and family.

Babysitter

Most grandparents would admit that the expectation they are most often confronted with is babysitting. I found that babysitting became a daily job for grandmothers because they are always available to bless their grandchildren with inexpensive childcare. It is not always something a grandparent desires or is equipped to handle. Babysitting, even with grandchildren, is sometimes a chore and an inconvenience, and I do not recommend allowing it to grow into a habit. When babysitting is demanded of us, honesty is paramount. There should be an understanding from the beginning that you are free to say "no" when you can't or don't want to watch the little ones. As in all relationships, communication will go a long way to help avoid conflicts.

Babysitting can be a time to bless the parents and also bless the grandchildren. We should see it as an opportunity to build love, faith, and wisdom into our legacy and their future.

Rule Follower

There is a saying that goes, **"What happens at Grandma's house stays at Grandma's house."** Unfortunately, we hear all too often that grandparents feel they can do whatever they please because they are grandparents. But part of our job description should be to uphold the rules the parents have set in place. We need to be rule followers, not rule breakers.

Teaching a child that he or she can break the parents' rules when they aren't looking can come back to haunt us, damage the relationship between the child and his parents, and ultimately harm the child we dearly love.

We must respect the hard-and-fast rules our parents have set down. With other rules, we can be slightly lenient if we discuss it with the parents.

Whenever a parent breaks the parental rules at our

house, we make sure to confess our transgression at the first opportunity. If it was something we planned ahead of time, like keeping them up past their normal bedtime for a special activity, we would ask permission beforehand and explain our reasoning.
In any case, we are careful to be totally honest with the parents. In that way, we honor their position and show the children that they must honor their father and mother as God has commanded.
We must remember that we are secondary in the lives of our grandchildren, and their parents are primary.

Story-Teller

Grandparents have many stories to share, so it's natural for them to tell their grandchildren. Through this, we can delight future generations with tales of our past and the lessons we learned through mistakes and successes. Some parents believe it's important to talk about God as often as possible. Grandchildren love to hear how God answers prayers, changes our hearts, or saves us from disasters.
They appreciate it when we learn to tell the wonderful old biblical stories in a new and fresh way, as we see them again through the young eyes of the next generation.
We also tell stories about our childhood friends and other adventures and

activities from our younger years, and our granddaughters and grandsons are amazed to hear them.
They often keep asking us for "one more story" about our childhood.

Even our older grandchildren have asked for those stories.
Recently, they asked about love interests we had before we found each other. The big question they finally asked was, "How did you know when you found the right one?" That's a notable example of how stories often lead to discussions about life lessons and character issues.
Books chosen carefully tell stories that can also trigger good conversations. We love

reading with our grandchildren—reading a story to them or having them read to us. Literature, whether old favorites or new finds, can tell stories that resonate with young and old. In this age of TV, videos, computers, and apps, it may take some coaxing to get them to sit and listen, but I have found that if you start young, they will remain interested when they sense a good story is in the air.

Memory-Maker

How will your grandchildren remember you? Were you the grandpa who took them fishing, on long walks, or out in the yard to look up at the stars? Could you be the grandma who bakes the cookies or makes a pot of homemade soup?

They should be holidays where all family members come together to celebrate, like Christmas. Celebrations are filled with new and exciting activities wrapped up in long-held traditions. Our grandchildren come to the house expecting to have fun, and we try not to disappoint. These kinds of memories and traditions are the best kind of inheritance we can leave to our descendants—even better than money or possessions. Of far more value are a godly birthright, important life lessons that will get them through life and save them untold problems, a deep and practical knowledge of the Scriptures, and a sense of family continuity.

Memories help give them roots.

Grandparents tell the stories that root children in family history and faith history. Children must deal with rapid changes at home, at school, and even inside their developing bodies. It is reassuring for them to know they are part of a larger, continuing story—the story of faith and family. Memory-makers leave a legacy.

Faith-Builder

3 John 4 is one of my favorite Scripture verses. It says: "I have no greater joy than to hear that my children are walking in the truth." Of course, I'm also thinking about my grandchildren when I read

that verse. Sharing our faith helps it to grow in us and plants seeds that will grow in our grandchildren. Prayer should always be our first step in helping them build trust in God. Through prayer, we can seek the direction of the Holy Spirit and lead our loved ones closer to the Father by using our aged wisdom from a foundational faith, clothed with a listening ear. Being an effective grandparent includes having a vulnerable, honest, and loving heart. As faith-builders, we will listen carefully to the hearts of our children and grandchildren, which is crucial to knowing how to respond as we seek to build up, not tear down. Also, our ongoing presence in our grandchildren's lives can help them grow as Jesus grew "in wisdom and stature, and in favor with God and man" (Luke 2:52). Our roles can be important puzzle pieces to help complete the picture of a healthy, growing family.

So, what is our job description? We help to fill in the gaps between the generations.

We provide connections between the future and the past (and our grandchildren do want to be connected). We take our roles seriously and work at them the best we can. We do have an important role to play.

Chapter 7

Roles of the Aunty/Uncle

An aunt is the female sibling of a mother or father, but knowing what an aunt is and what her responsibilities are two very different things.
In African culture, which tends to put the nuclear family at its center, the responsibilities of an aunt are largely undefined. But among more collective cultures, such as American, Hispanic, and Asian cultures, the aunt's role is much more demanding and defined. Regardless of cultural differences and norms, there are several important things any aunt should be prepared to do.

The face of the so-called "African" family is rapidly changing, and with such change comes different roles for family members.

As families are busy with work or going on a vacation, often a female relative, such as an aunt, may be called upon to provide female influence and companionship to children.

Additionally, with huge numbers of immigrant families now living in the U.S., those families bring with them their particular culture's roles for aunts and other extended family members.

But regardless of whether you've got kids, these are the kinds of roles that aunts and uncles can play:

The "Cool" Adult

You have different life experiences than your nieces and nephews' parents, which makes you cool right off the bat. Free of the responsibility of the parenting role, you allow the kid in you to come out. When adults reflect back on their aunts and uncles, having fun with them is often among the top memories.

Confidant and Trusted Adviser

Kids often say they can talk to aunts and uncles about things they are uncomfortable talking to their parents about. You can add a different perspective, and they may be open to telling you things and listening to your advice when they really need it but don't want to talk to their parents—*if* they can trust you.

Extra Provider

I hear a lot about aunts and uncles who provide

"extras" for their nieces and nephews, such as an aunt who makes doll clothes or provides spending money for a special trip; an uncle who pays for rock climbing lessons or buys a wedding dress.

These extras can make nieces and nephews feel so special and can even shape their life experiences. You may also provide the extra funds to cover education, housing, or important purchases for them.

Role Model

These days, more than ever, children are influenced by the media and their friends—not always positive role models.

You give your nieces and nephews alternative examples of family, career, relationships, hobbies, and values. You will teach them more by how you live than you ever could by talking to them.

Family Compadre

Because you have the same family — and you've known their parents all or most of your life — you might share their frustrations or understand their viewpoint more than anyone else does. Being familiar but somewhat outside the situation when conflicts with parents arise can be a plus. Kids may listen to you in a way they won't listen to their parents, and you may even be able to play a mediator or peacemaker role in the family.

Surrogate Parent
When mom and dad are busy or away, aunts and uncles can help fill the gap with extra attention, interest, and affection, as well as practical help such as making meals, taking kids to appointments, or helping with homework.

Cheerleader
You keep up with their activities and goals; triumphs and failures. You don't assume — you *ask* how you can support them and are prepared to follow through. When they are experiencing disapproval from others, you find something to love about them. You are their fan, and they know it.

How to Bond with Nieces and Nephews

Be open. Listen more than you talk and be empathetic; don't push and be as neutral as possible.
Be trustworthy. Be clear that you will keep their confidence to yourself—*unless* they are in danger. Let their parents know that is your plan.
Be in touch. Text, call, Facebook, Skype—do whatever it takes to touch base frequently.
Be responsive. Offer to help, and actively respond when asked to do something.
Be available. Go to their school and sports or other extracurricular events, shopping trips, prom night, births and birthdays,

weddings, firsts and other life milestones.

Be fun. You have the opportunity to be a fun aunt or uncle—take it!

Be interested. Meet them at their level and find out their interests. Learn about their hobbies and activities. "Cheer them on!

Be yourself. Just be who you are. Nix the preaching and instructing—it won't work. You'll influence them most by how you live.

Be the bonus. If you can, help out with those little "extras" that can make big differences in their lives.

Be the receiver. Let them have the confidence booster and fun of helping you with things, too. Listen to their advice — it's a reciprocal relationship.

Overall, motherhood requires a lot of work in the life of every woman, regardless of whether she is legally married, a single parent, a grandmother, an aunt, or an uncle. It encompasses everything and gives us a sense of belonging by teaching us to love ourselves before we can love another person (your child).

www.ingramcontent.com/pod-product-compliance
Lightning Source LLC
LaVergne TN
LVHW010506160826
845677LV00012B/2693

* 9 7 9 8 8 4 4 1 5 3 8 4 6 *